Featherstone

# PRESS IT, SWITCH IT,
## TURN IT, MOVE IT!

Providing high quality early ICT experiences

Published 2013 by Featherstone Education
Bloomsbury Publishing Plc
50 Bedford Square, London, WC1B 3DP
www.bloomsbury.com

ISBN 978-1-4081-9505-5

Text © Terry Gould 2013
Design © Lynda Murray
Photos on pages: 9, 17, 25, 29, 33, 34, 35, 42, 45, 49, 51, 53, 54 and 55
© Shutterstock
Grateful thanks are offered to TTS Group Ltd, who have provided the main image
for the cover and images for the inside pages in this publication.

A CIP catalogue for this book is available from the British Library.

Printed and bound in India by Replika Press Pvt. Ltd

1   3   5   7   9   10   8   6   4   2

This book is produced using paper that is made from wood grown in managed,
sustainable forests. It is natural, renewable and recyclable. The logging and
manufacturing process conform to the environmental regulations of the country
of origin.

To see our full range of titles visit www.bloomsbury.com

Thank you to all the children and practitioners whose images appear in this
book with special mention to: Alma Park Primary School, Manchester; Medlock
Primary School, Manchester; Acorn Childcare Ltd and the London Early Years
Foundation.

# Contents

# Introduction

Information and Communication Technology (ICT) is much more than simply being about computers. The importance of ICT in the lives of young children cannot be overstated and there is little doubt that the future for all children will involve ICT at a level that perhaps none of us can yet comprehend. Hence, ICT skills developed today, along with a keen interest in ICT, are likely to lead to workplace skills of the future. But for the present (the 'today' in the life of a child in the Early Years Foundation Stage) these are the skills and interests that will help them to engage in playful learning through early ICT.

ICT opens doors and creates possibilities for the active young child and can be particularly supportive of a wide range of early communication and language skills and thinking skills. Indeed, high quality ICT experiences can support all the other Early Learning Goals (prime and specific) in exciting ways, including writing, mathematics and expressive arts and design, and can be strongly linked with the newly recognised characteristics of effective learning.

ICT should enable practitioners, through its effective use, to support and enhance all children's learning and development. It should:

- **develop strong and effective good practice with all children**

- **engage, motivate and inspire young children**

- **support all aspects of the seven areas learning and development both indoors and outdoors**

- **support exploration, experimentation, decision making and independent learning**

- **promote and extend opportunities for child-initiated and independent learning**

- **challenge stereotypes and develop positive images of young children irrespective of any learning difficulties.**

This book also recognises the challenges facing practitioners and the notion that unless we develop effective partnerships between home and schools or settings then what children achieve is always likely to be less than it could be otherwise.

It acknowledges the growing efforts being made by parents in the home to provide for children's early learning and development and the new requirements of the revised EYFS for even stronger partnerships with parents that impact on improved outcomes for children.

**Terry Gould**

July 2013

PRESS IT, SWITCH IT, TURN IT, MOVE IT!

# Chapter 1

# ICT and the revised Early Years Foundation Stage

> **Children recognise that a range of technology is used in places such as homes and schools. They select and use technology for particular purposes.**
>
> *Statutory Framework for the Early Years Foundation Stage 2012*

Within the revised EYFS (2012) the areas of learning and development have been extended from six to seven but the number of Early Learning Goals has been reduced from 69 to just 17. Technology remains under the specific area of Understanding the World (which was formerly Knowledge and Understanding of the World). However, the use of technology can be linked to support for learning and development in each of the seven areas of learning and with each of the other 16 Early Learning Goals.

The single technology Early Learning Goal in the revised framework states that 'Children recognise that a range of technology is used in places such as homes and schools. They select and use technology for particular purposes.'

Development Matters guidance indicates that early ICT for children from birth up to and around 20 months is very much about them 'exploring and making sense of objects and how they behave.' (*Development Matters in the Early Years Foundation Stage* 2012)

As children grow and develop from around 16 months up to 26 months the guidance states that generally children will begin to show a much more developed interest in 'toys with buttons, flaps and simple mechanisms' which they can press, turn, switch or move as they begin to learn to operate these and also will begin to anticipate repeated sounds, sights and actions.

So, prior to the next, 22 to 36 month stage referred to in Development Matters is the period which I shall term 'the baby and toddler stage'. At this age we need to understand that ICT is all around very young children and that even the youngest of these will begin to notice its effects and uses.

Babies and toddlers will notice others, often adults but also children, using ICT to:

- **communicate their ideas**

- **to control items in their world**

- **to engage in play through it.**

Naturally, babies and toddlers will want to explore and investigate toys that make sounds, light up or move but it is of the greatest importance that whatever and wherever we allow children to touch or otherwise engage with toys and devices it is safe for them to do so.

They will use their senses including their mouths to explore and investigate so all objects need to be suitably clean and free from loose parts that they may swallow. We can provide for exploration and investigation for the very young child through the provision of treasure baskets which promote heuristic and sensory play. This can be later developed to include toys that can be pressed to create sound and/or movement such as mini keyboards and musical telephones. Practitioners can support

children through showing an interest and modelling their use, bearing in mind that children will want to repeat their experiences and successes many times.

Children from around 22 months up to the age of three (36 months), a period I shall call 'the pre-nursery class stage' begin to develop a greater understanding that they can operate simple toys or mechanisms by using the linked controls. At this stage control is very much experimental, but each experience provides with it increased skills and knowledge which will later develop into more clearly refined understanding.

As children from 36 months upwards move on, and in many cases begin to attend a nursery class in a school, their skills and knowledge begin to develop into transferable levels of understanding about what they can expect when they engage with early ICT. For example, they begin to understand that information can be retrieved from a computer and that images can be downloaded from a digital camera. When they are out in the locality they can press the button at a pelican crossing and know they will get a response if they do so.

At the age of 30 to 50 months children should know how to operate simple ICT equipment, such as a CD player, and they will begin to show an interest in technological toys as well as real ICT devices such as cameras and mobile phones. They know that information can be retrieved from computers and show developing skills in doing just that.

# Three strands of early ICT

Practitioners should develop their own understanding that there are three interrelated 'strands or elements' of the specific early ICT Early Learning Goal: 'Children recognise that a range of technology is used in places such as homes and schools. They select and use technology for particular purposes.' which they need to pursue, at an appropriate developmental level.

These three strands or elements are:

**1) Develop an awareness and use of everyday technology in the real world.**

**2) Use ICT equipment to support their learning.**

**3) Use simple switch, remote control and programmable toys (electronic or battery operated).**

These are each linked to the requirements of the revised EYFS framework including the characteristics of effective learning, the new Early Learning Goals, the prime and specific areas of learning and development, and the four principles of the Unique Child, Enabling Environments, Positive Relationships and Learning and Development.

**1** Are children developing an awareness and use of everyday technology in the real world?

Things to consider in this element are:

◆ Level 1

Can children identify name and talk about the technology which they have come into contact with in the world around them? This could include: CD players, telephones, mobile phones, ipods, ipads, microwave cookers and vacuum cleaners.

● Level 2

Have children developed their skills to be able to operate and use everyday technology? This could include items like a vacuum cleaner, television or CD player.

● Level 3

Have children shown an awareness of the more complex use of technology in the environment? This could include such items as a pedestrian crossing, a cash point dispenser or a webcam.

**2** Do children effectively use ICT equipment to support their learning?

Things to consider developmentally within this element are:

◆ **Level 1**

**Do children show an interest in using ICT equipment such as cameras, computers or voice recorders? This might include taking pictures or using a touch screen.**

◆ **Level 2**

**Are the children developing their ability to use more complex equipment with some adult support? For example, making a DVD or video recording, using a talking book program on a computer or downloading images from a digital camera.**

◆ **Level 3**

**Are children able to make progress to becoming independent users of equipment for a specific purpose? This might include clicking on an icon on a computer screen and accessing a software program, taking pictures with a camera to support making passports for the role-play area or using apps (applications) on an ipad.**

**3** Are children able to use simple switch, remote control and programmable toys (electronic or battery operated)?

Things to consider in this element are:

◆ **Level 1**

Do children show an interest in switch, remote control or programmable toys and devices? This could be a ball that lights up when pressed or equipment where a tune is played when a button is pressed.

◆ **Level 2**

Are children gradually developing their skills to independently use switch, remote control or programmable toys and devices? They may still need some adult or peer support. It can be a switch on a control pad to make a toy move or make a sound or a specific button on a remote handset to operate a CD, DVD or television.

◆ **Level 3**

Do children demonstrate their independent ability to use toys and devices purposefully in their play? This might be using a remote control car, a mini programmable robot or a metal detector.

# Chapter 2

# Early ICT and the prime and specific areas of learning

> **Early years practitioners have a big part to play in influencing the continuing social development of the child. Collaborative work involving ICT in all its forms may offer new opportunities for doing this.**
>
> *Cooper and Brna* 2002

In the revised EYFS (2012) the seven areas of learning are split into prime and specific areas. It is important that practitioners effectively plan how to use ICT to support each area of learning. This chapter aims to support practitioners in this task.

## Prime areas

The revised prime areas of learning and development are:

1 **Personal, Social and Emotional Development**

2 **Physical Development**

3 **Communication and Language.**

## 1 Personal, Social and Emotional Development

This covers the aspects of :

■ **Making relationships**

■ **Self-confidence and self-awareness**

■ **Managing feelings and behaviour**

Remote control toys and devices, computer programs and programmable toys can be powerful facilitators of opportunities for children to work together collaboratively. They can offer children challenges that stimulate and support their personal, social and emotional development.

◆ In using a listening centre alongside other children, in waiting their turn to use the mouse or the roller ball or in working on a group task with a programmable toy, children are often highly motivated to develop personal and social skills such as sharing and turn taking, shared enjoyment and genuine excitement in learning.

◆ Using ICT equipment puts the child in control, offering a sense of autonomy. A trial and error approach is often adopted and it seems safe to make mistakes.

◆ Through ICT children frequently face problem-solving opportunities. Open-ended activities encourage children to initiate and try out new ideas. Being in control of their own success along with immediate positive feedback provided by ICT toys, devices and software, builds personal confidence and self-esteem.

◆ Children correctly handling ICT equipment begin to develop an understanding of shared responsibility, a respect for things, sensitivity to the needs and views of each other, a sense of justice and a sense of right and wrong.

◆ Digital images can help to broaden children's cultural awareness and experiences within the context of development in other areas of the curriculum and also an awareness of equality of opportunity through positive images of gender, race and disability.

◆ Children can be supported to begin to learn about the diversity of need and the importance of an inclusive world.

◆ Practitioners can support this awareness through the ways they adapt existing ICT resources and provide additional supporting materials and devices to ensure that all children can access learning opportunities.

## 2 Physical Development

This covers the aspects of:

- **Moving and handling**

- **Health and self-care**

The use of ICT can support many aspects of physical development particularly in the area of fine motor control. Ways in which ICT particularly supports this area of development include:

◆ Using ICT devices which help to develop fine motor control and hand eye co-ordination, for example a mouse, metal detector, mini robots and remote control cars.

◆ ICT devices being made available for children to handle in their spontaneous play, such as a toy scanner in a shop or a mobile phone or walkie-talkie outdoors which will encourage children to mimic the dexterous manipulation observed in adults around them. This offers practice without fear of failure and children's confidence will grow as they develop familiarity with the range of ICT devices and equipment continuously and regularly available to them.

◆ Through using a new computer program, device or ICT toy, which has a high novelty value, children will be highly motivated to explore it independently.

◆ Practitioners should give careful consideration to the match between the child's development and the degree of dexterity demanded by the device, toy or software. For instance a touch screen monitor can be used to provide access to the computer for very young children, or those whose physical capacity is limited.

◆ Clear coloured labelling of significant keys of the standard keyboard should be considered, as should the provision of alternatives to the standard keyboard e.g. BigKeys.

◆ Alternatives to a standard mouse, which are easier for some children to use to operate programs, should also be considered, for example with a switch device.

◆ Practitioners need to be aware that software is likely to vary in the demands it makes on a child's physical control, so a child who has just developed the ability to use the mouse to click on an icon will be challenged by a program requiring the user to drag and drop.

◆ The provision of sound mats which help children explore how their movements can be used to create different sounds.

◆ The use of CD or cassette tape players to support music and dance type activities both indoors and outdoors.

◆ Supporting non-walking children to use their electric wheelchairs to dance to a variety of styles of music by operating the controls of their wheelchairs.

◆ The use of computer software which can be used to support health and bodily awareness.

## ③ Communication and Language

- **Listening and attention**

- **Understanding**

- **Speaking**

This area of learning can be supported through ICT when:

◆ There is a good range of software or internet programs available to children that offer them access to a wide range of stories, rhymes and songs in new and different forms. This should enable children to be in control and able to enjoy listening to the text at a speed which suits them.

◆ Many software programs are interactive and allow children to explore the full range of possibilities, for example making characters in a picture 'speak' and/or move, looking in cupboards and opening doors and so on. One good example of this is 'Mouse In The House' by d2 Digital by Design.

◆ Interactive whiteboards (IWBs) are used effectively in settings both for independent use by children and for planned adult-led activities.

◆ ICT is effective in supporting the development of communication and language through the use of appropriate software programs. These include programs which support and encourage children to meaningfully engage with stories, songs and rhymes, such as book CD ROMS, pre-recorded stories, or screened big books as well as quality educational broadcasts.

◆ ICT provides support for young children who have the stories to tell but lack the transcribing skills to record these independently, for example, recording children's own stories and responses with the practitioner acting as a scribe using desktop publishing or interactive software. This supports children to create stories including developing their descriptive language.

# Specific areas

The revised specific areas of development (2012) are:

1 **Literacy**

2 **Mathematics**

3 **Understanding the World**

4 **Expressive Arts and Design**

1 **Literacy**

This covers the aspects of:

▪ **Reading**

▪ **Writing**

This area of learning can be supported through ICT when there is a good range of software and internet programs available to children that offer them access to a wide range of reading and writing skills.

◆ This should enable children to be in control and to enjoy the text at a speed which suits them, go back if they wish, have the words highlighted as they read, 'speak' and/or move, look in cupboards and open doors and so on.

◆ IWBs are used effectively in settings both for independent use by children for reading and writing purposes – in both child-initiated and adult-led activities.

◆ ICT is effective in supporting the development of literacy through the use of software programs that develop reading and writing skills. These include those that reinforce letter and sound correspondence and those which support and encourage children to meaningfully engage with stories, songs and rhymes, such as book CD ROMS, pre-recorded stories, on-screen big books as well as quality educational broadcasts.

◆ A number of software packages and/or online resources are skilfully designed to help children recognise letters and words. Often they are interactive and highly motivational.

## ② Mathematics

This covers the aspects of:

- **Numbers**

- **Shape, space and measures**

Mathematical learning has the potential to be greatly supported through the use of ICT. This can be facilitated by:

◆ ICT software or websites helping to develop children's concept of shape, pattern and sequencing. Such programs can be useful in reinforcing learning which takes place in the creative workshop area, the maths area and the construction area.

◆ ICT packages, created to support the development of sorting and matching skills, and to help to reinforce the ideas and concepts developed in first-hand practical experiences.

◆ ICT activities, which help to develop and reinforce the concept of number. Children can move the programmable toys in different directions: forwards, backwards, left or right. A mini floor robot can travel around the room or on a floor mat.

◆ Software programs or websites which include number recognition tasks. Many of these involve the concept of order 1st, 2nd, 3rd and so on and often progress to concepts such as more/less and simple addition/subtraction.

◆ Easy to use digital cameras being effectively used with very young children including being utilised to make pattern, size, number and sequence books. For example images taken (by the adult and/or child) of models which are tall or short being used to reinforce this concept, or photographs taken of different routines of the day made into a visual timetable to reinforce the concept of sequence, or pictures taken of patterns created by the children and used to support attempts to recreate these.

◆ Children being able to enter data into simple data charts such as bar graphs.

## ③ Understanding the World

This covers the aspects of:

- **People and communities**

- **The world**

- **Technology**

◆ ICT can help children become involved in exploration and investigation of the world around them.

◆ Software and other internet-based resources can support and enhance specific knowledge about aspects of 'people and communities' and 'the world'. Children can be stimulated and encouraged through these to talk about their own home and community life and the experiences of others.

◆ Technology can also be used to make class or group books about activities and experiences in the school or setting including trips out and visitors in.

◆ Practitioners can invite children and families with experience of living in other countries to bring in photographs and objects.

◆ The use of DVD players, video recorders and IWBs to play short clips of film which support children's knowledge of the world can have a significant impact on children's learning and motivation. They can be supported and encouraged to discuss what they have watched but can also record their own clips of things they have engaged with and experienced.

◆ Role-play ICT in such scenarios as a doctor's surgery, a builder's yard, a post office or a café – where items such a telephone, a till or a microwave are used help children to build up a greater awareness of how ICT is used in the world around them.

◆ A visualiser can be used to project images from books on communities and different cultures and other items of interest through an IWB.

◆ ICT learning walks where such things as automatics telling machines or cash points (ATMs), traffic lights and satellite dishes can be seen first-hand in use and which will support children's knowledge of ICT in the world in a range of ways.

## ④ Expressive Arts and Design

This covers the aspects of:

■ **Exploring and using media and materials**

■ **Being imaginative**

◆ ICT can be a powerful tool in supporting the development of children's creativity, particularly where it involves sound and colour media materials. To support this area of learning and development particular attention should be given to developing aspects of the learning environment which reflects this.

◆ A learning environment which is ICT rich will greatly support and help to broaden the use of children's imagination and creativity through such things as music making, dance, role-play and story making.

◆ Children should be provided with independent access to a CD player or recorder and be able to select and listen to stories, songs, poems and rhymes as well as being able to use this to record their own sounds: such as playing an instrument or singing.

◆ Software which encourages children to create patterns and to 'draw' using screen tools supports and fosters their artistic talents and allows them to express their creativity. Through such software children are able to explore colour, shape and texture in two and three dimensions.

◆ Music making software or mini keyboards allow children to succeed in composing and exploring sounds. Some programs will introduce children to a wider range of instruments than they would normally have available to them including those from across cultures.

◆ Even where children do not directly use the ICT themselves it can be a catalyst for creativity. For example a CD player for music and movement or digital images to inspire them to talk about and maybe write about things they have done can then be shown through an IWB or projector.

◆ Multimedia programs which allow sound to be added are now common place and easier to use. These will add a further dimension to the learning experience. With some adult skills to support them, the experience can be recorded of images with accompanying sound and this will involve three senses coming together: visual, auditory and tactile.

# Chapter 3

# Creating an ICT-rich early learning environment

Good early years practitioners with basic ICT knowledge will be able to spot opportunities where ICT can be used to capitalise on what interests and enthuses children. With ICT resources now being so readily and affordably available, planning for ICT should not be a bolt on part but an implicit element of any EYFS educational programme that seeks to maximise children's capacity and potential as learners.

Always consider ways in which ICT can be incorporated into your existing provision or used to enhance it further. Clearly the message in the revised EYFS is that ICT is much more than merely a case of providing a few computers and setting up drill and skill type activities for the children.

The revised EYFS continues to indicate the importance of a high quality learning environment, both indoors and outdoors, which can support child-initiated and adult-led learning and development opportunities. It stresses the significant impact that the learning environment can have on the young child's learning and development and their motivation to engage with elements within this. This learning environment must include suitable age-appropriate ICT resources and equipment.

In order to be able to create such an environment it is important that practitioners are aware of:

- **the wide range of ICT resources and equipment currently available**

- **how these resources can be most effectively used within the learning environment**

- **how best these resources can be used to support adult-led activities as well as opportunities for children to use them independently and safely**

- **the potential of all developed spaces and areas to include and involve early ICT opportunities and activities.**

There are some other philosophical and principled considerations to be taken into account when purchasing ICT software and other resources.

These are:

→ **Will the child be in control and able to make independent choices about the use they make of the resources or equipment?**

→ **Do the resources/equipment encourage collaboration?**

→ **Are they of a suitably high educational value that supports and enhances children's learning and development?**

→ **Can the use of items/resources/equipment be fully embedded and used meaningfully and purposefully by the children?**

→ **Are the applications involved both intuitive and transparent?**

→ **Have you ensured that any images contained (for example, in software or on a website) do not contain stereotypes or violence?**

Early ICT resources and equipment can be loosely grouped under three headings although there are many examples of overlap between these. Settings and schools should have an appropriate level of resources/equipment under each heading.

1. Communication: **This can include a karaoke machine, cameras, talking tins, microphones and so on.**

2. Role-play: **This can include a cooker, iron, kettle, microwave, vacuum cleaner and so on.**

3. Control/programmable: **This can include programmable mini robots, a Pixie or Roamer, a remote control vehicle, a computer or IWB.**

# Indoors

Practitioners on a budget need to consider which ICT resources to include and where. Ideas here consider each of the play areas within an early years setting and consider which ICT resources could be provided. Due to limitations of space and budgets not all provisions will have all of these areas set up and this should not be a concern, as long as the setting can demonstrate that they are providing support for all seven areas of learning and development through the areas they do provide.

## ICT and the book area

- This developed space could include books which the children have made themselves, often with the help of practitioners, using computer desktop software. These would contain digital images and computerised text.

- Books with buttons to press to make sounds of animals or transport which encourage an early interest in reading through both their visual and auditory senses could be provided.

- Talking photo albums which can be recorded in the setting, and often in different languages can be made into a variety of books linked to a topic, children's interests or aspects which support areas of their learning such as phonic alphabet books, tricky word books and so on.

- Where the book area is turned into a den or cave to link in with a theme or predicted interest then torches can be provided for the children to explore the texts and images in the books or talking photo albums.

## ICT and the listening area

- This developed space should have access to a stage appropriate CD player which is easy for the child to operate and suitable headphones (ideally remote type).

- Headphones need to be checked regularly to ensure they are working effectively and not adjusted to too high a volume.

- In this space children can listen to a range of songs, rhymes, poems and good quality storybooks (some can be home-made). Some recordings will be commercial and others made by staff or parents or children at the school or setting.

- In some listening spaces, staff provide things for children to listen to such as small electronic musical instruments and toys.

- The books selected for the children to listen to can be linked to those suggested in *Early Literacy Fundamentals: A Balanced Approach to Language, Listening and Literacy Skills: Ages 3 to 6* by Sue Palmer and Ros Bayley (Pembroke Publishing Ltd 2005).

## ICT and the drawing and writing area

- In this area children could use a desktop computer or a laptop for word processing.

- It might contain 'play' office equipment such as a fax machine, photocopier or phone.

- Recordable postcards might be included where children can both write and record the message/questions verbally.

- There could be writing frameworks for children to create emails or faxes to be sent.

## ICT and the small world area

- This area is able to offer a meaningful environment for the use of small remote control cars and other vehicles, Bee-Bot mini robots, LEGO Builder Bots or other devices.

- It also is an ideal place for children to engage with calming creatures2 which have realistic breathing movements and sounds when stroked, for example, pretend puppies.

## ICT and the song and rhyme/ performing arts area

- A suitably robust and easy to use CD player/ recorder with microphone is ideal to include in this area as it will allow children to listen to and join in singing pre-recorded songs and rhymes, as well recording their own versions.

- A karaoke machine with a CD player incorporated is also a great asset, this need to be child friendly and robust.

- The pre-writing programme in *Write Dance in the Early Years* by Ragnhild Oussoren (Sage Publications 2012) can also be used with small groups to introduce handwriting to young children through dance and music.

- Child can access music and movement sessions on a child-initiated/independent basis using a range of equipment provided.

- Floor-based keyboards as well as mini table top keyboards are also useful additions to this area.

## ICT and the role-play area

- This space can provide play opportunities which involve meaningful and relevant experiences to use ICT. This will support children developing their ability and confidence to use technology and their awareness of its use in everyday life.

- It is useful to use models of equipment, toy replicas and old equipment which no longer functions (do remember to cut off the wires and plugs). However, the use of some working ICT equipment is also beneficial to include such as a radio or CD player.

- Adults need to engage in modelling how to use ICT and you can do this by spending time interacting with the children in the role-play area.

- Children's own ideas should be considered when setting up role-play areas and practitioners should seek to discuss with them which types of equipment to include, such as an electronic baby scales in a baby clinic.

## ICT and the construction area

- This developed space can support children's skills and understanding of construction, building and de-constructing.

- Builder's mini toy replica tools can be useful in supporting imaginative play, for example so the children can pretend to be a joiner or plumber.

- LEGO Builder Bots are also a useful resources for this area.

- Provide a 'tinkering box' of old ICT objects to take apart and try to put back together: remember to risk assess all parts are safe for the children to do this.

- Have a digital camera handy to support children recording their play and activity in this area.

## ICT and the creative workshop area

- Use of light boxes can work well within this area.

- Children can use light boxes to explore and create patterns and designs with a wide range of natural, made and found resources: you will need a power point nearby.

- Having a digital camera handy will also support children in recording their expressive and creative ideas in this area.

## ICT and the maths area

- ICT resources in this area will support pattern, shape and number, estimation, direction time and measurement of distance and size.

- This will often be approached in ways which engage children in problem solving.

- Floor mats that make sounds and others that offer maths challenges can be very engaging for children.

- Talking photo books made into number and pattern books are ideal.

- Provide Bee-Bot mini robots and floor mats or Perspex boards (minimum thickness of 4 mm) which support children thinking and programming skills in this area or in a space close by.

- Light boxes which support children experimenting with patterns are also suitable to include: you will need a power point nearby.

- A lap top, an ipad or desktop computer can be included with the mathematics based activities on offer.

## ICT and the water area

- Subject to size limitations of the water tray, there could be water craft included such as mini hovercrafts, remote control boats, and mini submarines. These need to be stage appropriate and risk assessment of situations must be made.

A key question might be how useful is a tiny water tray in reality? My suggestion is that you go for the biggest stage appropriate water tray you can afford and accommodate.

## ICT and the sand area

■ Depending on the size of the sand tray or sand pit this area can be used in a variety of different ways with metal detectors including mini hand hold typos.

Again a key question might be how useful is a tiny sand tray in reality? My suggestion is that you go for the biggest stage appropriate sand tray you can afford and accommodate and I would always recommend a floor based sand pit space allowing at least 200 mm x 1200 mm or even bigger. This will allow so much more versatility and variety of use.

## ICT and the investigation/exploration area

◆ This area needs to support and encourage children's natural desire to explore and investigate enabling them to find things out and then record their findings.

◆ It could include items which help this to take place such as a digital camera, an Easi-Scope magnifier or recorder, torches, sound and light toys, simple microscopes or electronic magnifying lenses.

◆ A light box could also be useful here with stage appropriate resources: you will need a power point nearby.

## ICT and the malleable area

■ To ensure we encourage creativity and thinking skills practitioners should consider the addition of a play microwave oven and or cooker and mini electronic timers in this area.

## ICT and the sensory area

◆ This area will need to provide a range of light and sound stimulating resources and equipment.

◆ It could involve resources that have switches and buttons and which encourage children to interact with the resources in different ways so that they begin to learn about cause and effect through their play.

## The ICT area

■ As we have seen ICT will be everywhere and anywhere, in most areas of the early years environment. A specific ICT area may well be the place where computers/laptops are mainly stored along with items such as Bee Bots, I Bugs and remote control cars which can then be used in other areas.

■ The ICT area can be home to a wide range of hardware such as IWBs, printers, speakers and so on too.

# Outdoors

When using ICT outdoors it is most important that the resources:

- **Are compatible with the nature of the space and how it is/can be used.**

- **Challenge children to develop their thinking through independent learning.**

- **Allow children to problem solve and be creative and imaginative.**

- **Are provided within a routine which allows children's play not to be interrupted for suitably long periods.**

- **Are not a bolt on part but an integral component of the play experience.**

- **Are suitably robust and waterproof to be durable in their use outdoors.**

- **Have been modelled and supported by how best to maintain their longevity of use.**

Outdoor learning opportunities can and should provide a different scale of activities which, according to Woodbridge, is often 'bigger, bolder, messier and noisier.' All practitioners certainly need to consider the fact that through quality outdoor learning experiences children will be accessing their learning and development in different ways than they might do indoors.

For many children the outdoors environment provides a feeling of being free and able to move without some of the restrictions of indoors and limited space. It almost always brings with it a greater awareness of the natural world including the weather and the seasons.

Using technology outdoors can often best be achieved with equipment that is already familiar to both the practitioner and the children. Digital cameras are an excellent resource to use as are metal detectors, DVD players and recorders, large remote control cars, walkie talkies, music mats or digital microscopes. Much will depend on the children's existing knowledge and experiences.

On the following pages are some examples of ICT resources and equipment that can be used outdoors. These have been linked to specific developed areas.

## ICT and the roadway area

This area can support role-play through such ICT items as:

- **petrol pumps (commercial or made)**

- **traffic lights (commercial or made)**

- **speed cameras (commercial or made)**

- **digital head cameras**

- **walkie talkies (commercial or made).**

## ICT and the natural materials area (sand, water, stones/pebbles)

In this space you can use:

- metal detectors (to find buried treasure and other metallic objects)

- mini electronic water pressure washers (to explore the power and use of water).

## ICT and the natural area (trees, grass, bushes)

This space lends itself to the use of:

- mini weather stations

- wireless outdoor bird box cameras.

## ICT and the construction area

Children will love to engage with:

- replica, play electronic tools that make realistic sounds such as Kango hammers and drills

- cement mixers.

## ICT and the imaginative play area

Imaginative play ICT items, as with the indoor role-play area, can be provided to good effect including:

- phones

- DVD players

- explorer's headlamps

- digital head cameras.

## Other outdoor equipment

Other items to consider using outdoors are:

- voice changer megaphones

- large remote controls cars/vehicles

- digital camcorders and still cameras

- mini hovercraft – great when an area outdoors is flooded!

- karaoke machine

- dance mats

- outdoor webcams

- Easi-Scope - magnifier recorder

- digital microscopes.

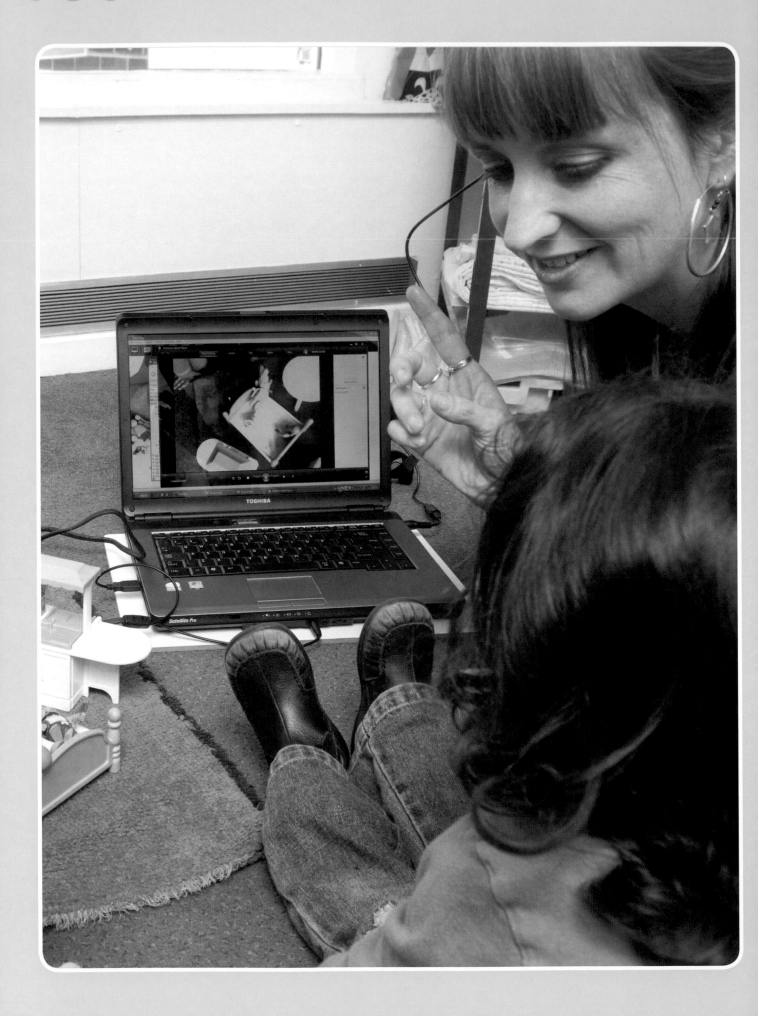

# Chapter 4

# The role of the adult and early ICT

> **Children need well informed adults who support children learning more effectively and from an earlier age as well as sufficient access to stage appropriate resources and experiences including those involving ICT.**
>
> *Gould* 2012

The role of the adult is a key part of the enabling environment for ICT. This role has many facets which include:

- **modelling**
- **facilitating and making possible**
- **scaffolding**
- **challenging**
- **enhancing**
- **inspiring interest and engagement**
- **providing positive feedback**
- **observing, assessing and effectively planning the next steps**
- **working in partnership with parents**
- **listening and responding to children**
- **recording progress made.**

# Observation, assessment and planning

Practitioners are required to plan a 'challenging and enjoyable experience for each child in all of the areas of learning and development.' (*Statutory Framework for the Eaely Years Foundation Stage, 2012*). This will involve them planning to support and enhance learning and development through planned play and other actively based learning – including that which relates to early ICT.

Observation of children should be at the heart of the planning process as without this we cannot be sure what children really know and understand and can do. The role of the adult is at the heart of the process of children's learning as it is the adults in a setting, working in partnership with parents and carers, that make it possible for the children to achieve their true potential.

Knowing the extent and the nature of children's response to, and their engagement with, early ICT allows adults to embrace this within their planning of the next steps for the child's future learning. Through planned and informal observations of children using ICT purposefully, practitioners can meet statutory assessment requirements by making accurate judgments about children's skills, knowledge and levels of understanding. When assessing in this way it is most important that all staff understand at an appropriate level that other areas of learning and development, other than merely those of technology, should be noted and used both formatively and summatively in appropriate ways.

# Providing and evaluating resources

Children should be provided with resources which they are able to use independently in purposeful ways. Before making a decision to purchase any resources or equipment practitioners should consider:

→ **how effective the item is in supporting learning and development?**

→ **what the maintenance costs are likely to be?**

→ **will the resource be durable in the hands of the young child?**

→ **which aspects of Development Matters or Early Learning Goals the activity could support?**

→ **will it fit with the four principles which underpin the EYFS?**

→ **what level of supervision or adult involvement will it need?**

→ **what stage of development will it best support?**

→ **whether it positively reflects gender, race or disability (if appropriate)**

→ **whether it promotes equality of opportunity**

→ **are there are any safety concerns?**

Many of these considerations cannot be made without having the item to physically trial before giving children access. If in doubt a request should be made for a purchase on a 'sale or return' basis. Alternatively, other local practitioners and settings who already have the resource or equipment could be consulted for feedback or opportunities to borrow and trial the resource explored.

# Health and safety considerations

Keeping children safe and healthy are key considerations under the statutory safeguarding and welfare requirements of the revised EYFS (2012).

Early ICT resources and equipment should be treated in the same way as any other resource/equipment with regards to health and safety considerations. They should be risk assessed and evaluated before use and children supported in using them appropriately. Practitioners should show children how to use resources and equipment safely and included within this is modelling the correct/appropriate way/s to use.

Staff should also monitor how long children sit in front of monitors and screens and place limits on this which are stage or age appropriate. They should also explain to children why any limits are being imposed and support children self regulating the time spent in front of screens and monitors.

Resources and equipment should be:

◆ **inspected on a daily and ongoing basis**

◆ **subject to a regular annual maintenance and safety check, completed by a competent contractor**

◆ **kept clean and in good working order.**

# ICT policy

Early years settings need to work towards an inclusive and transparent e-safety policy for ICT in the EYFS. It is important that any such policy should be appropriate for all children in the setting as well as clear and available so that parents and carers, as well as practitioners, understand how the policy will be reflected in consistent practice within the school or setting.

A policy should clearly reflect:

✓ **what is good practice**

✓ **how the school or setting delivers its aims and objectives in this area**

✓ **the ethos of the EYFS and its four underpinning principles.**

The aim of an e-safety policy for the use of ICT in the setting should be to protect the safety and welfare of children, their families and staff and it will operate under the umbrella of the Safeguarding and Welfare Policy.

It will need to outline how the school or setting has a total commitment to keeping children in their care safe and healthy when using ICT resources and equipment. Part of achieving this will be supporting all children to be aware of and to respond responsibly to any possible risks.

Where there is internet access provided the policy will need to identify how the filtering of content will be achieved as well how the overall content will be managed, including adherence to copyright law where this is applicable. Additionally, it will need to clarify how communication through email from the school or setting will be managed.

There may also be a need for a section on the staff use of social networking sites outside of their workplace.

# Partnership with parents and carers

The value and importance of a close working partnership with parent and carers is set out in the revised EYFS guidance framework. Parents and carers are recognised as the child's first and most enduring educator with a right to be consulted and informed about how their child is provided for within the EYFS and the progress they are making across all seven areas of learning and development.

It is important that practitioners provide parents and carers with information on the use and value of early ICT in the provision their child attends as well as how parents and carers can support their child in the home.

Parent's and carer's views and perspectives must also be sought and used so that an accurate and balanced view of the child is achieved.

Useful information for parents and carers often includes:

◆ **What ICT activities their child will be engaging with and how this will support their learning and development.**

◆ **What ICT resources and equipment children show an interest in and use to engage in their play and active learning.**

◆ **The type and range of ICT resources and equipment children may be using to support their learning and development.**

◆ **Ideas of how and when they can further support their child's ICT skills at home including how they can promote safety awareness with their child.**

◆ **How they can best share their child's ICT experiences outside the school or setting with staff and use this to work together to ensure practitioners there are able to effectively plan new and extended experiences for all children.**

# Chapter 5

# Using programmable toys and devices

> " Children learn and develop well in enabling environments, in which their experiences respond to their individual needs and there is a strong partnership between parents and/or carers.
>
> *Statutory Framework for the Early Years Foundation Stage 2012* "

The enabling environment principle is delivered through ICT by ensuring that children have access to:

★ **challenging and exciting resources**

★ **rich and stimulating learning opportunities**

★ **opportunities to explore and take risks and enjoy success.**

When providing activities involving programmable and controlled ICT equipment practitioners should reflect on:

◆ **what the children have gained in terms of skills and knowledge and understanding and what are the next steps for them**

◆ **how the equipment has motivated the children to be in control of their learning and to have intrinsic enjoyment through it**

◆ **how it has helped the children to achieve and learn something they would not have done without the use of ICT.**

Programmable toys and devices support a new dimension in children's learning and development and a large range of programmable toys or controllable robots are now available which are suitable for children in the EYFS. These include the Roamer, the Pixie the Pip and Bee Bots, without doubt the most modern and durable of these is the Bee Bot. Indeed many practitioners find these robot devices much easier for children to use as they are smaller lighter and less complex and have less buttons and are more appealing to the young eye than other devices.

Children will always need a short introduction to these toys or robots after which most will be able to engage independently and safely in exploring how they can be used and what they can do. By learning how to input instructions through pressing buttons, children have the opportunity to develop skills and knowledge in making things happen. To be successful in this type of programming activity there is a requirement that children have a certain level of understanding about number and direction. It is unlikely that most children under the age of three will have that necessary level of understanding but some of course will.

Programmable toys will enable children to engage in activities that will allow them to practise and refine their logical thought patterns as well as their skills of estimation number recognition, counting and sequencing.

Additionally they can be used to:

✓ **support learning by trial and error**

✓ **support creative thinking**

✓ **develop thinking and problem solving skills.**

To plan and programme a mini robot or toy children need to see the task from the point of view of the robot or toy. First of all this kind of challenging play encourages children to see things from different perspectives than they would otherwise. For example, to turn left depends which way you are starting from so for a child looking from a front perspective it will be different than a child looking from a back or rear perspective.

# Bee-Bot mini robot

Bee-Bots are robust mini robots that can be programmed to move in 150 mm/15 cm sized steps at a time either forwards backwards or to the left or right and complete turns in 90°. They have clear and bright buttons, a memory of up to 40 steps and sounds and flashing eyes to confirm instructions. The latest models are now rechargeable via a computer or a wall socket with a USB mains adaptor.

There are a great deal of accessories for the Bee-Bot which can be purchased including a wide variety of plastic floor mats such as street scenes, a map of the world, an alphabet chart, a number track, a seaside scene, a treasure map, a farm scene as well as jackets which can be character decorated, a trailer which simply hooks onto the back of your robot and is great for incorporating role-play and a range of 15 cm x 15 cm topic/theme card sets.

Using clear Perspex boards helps to stop the Bee-Bots movements becoming impaired or slowed as well as helping to ensure that the plastic mats keep flat on the floor or other surface. An ideal size for a Perspex board is 1200 mm x 600 mm x 4 mm thick (it is not advised to use any thinner than 4 mm for safety and durability reasons). These plain Perspex boards can be bought from large DIY stores and cost under £30 each. Once purchased they can either be left plain or marked into 150 mm squares using a permanent marker pen. Where a larger activity surface is required two of these boards can be laid side by side .

It is possible to purchase ready-made marked sheets on a roll which fit under these Bee-Bot boards, but a lower cost DIY option is to purchase 1000 gram decorator's lining paper (available in all DIY stores). This is slightly narrower than the 600 mm width of the Perspex boards but by overlapping two cut pieces at 1200 mm wide and then fixing them together using masking tape you can make it the right width and it will be thicker. You will then need to mark the squares on the lining paper.

The boards can be used in a variety of ways, here are three useful ideas:

## Theme cards activity

Affix the required pairs of topic/theme cards to some of the squares and then place the board over the sheet lining it up to the squares grid if necessary. Children can now send the Bee-Bot to 'collect' the matching pairs by programming it to do so. For example, if you are finding out about minibeasts then the picture cards could be pairs of minibeasts such as worms, bees, ladybirds, spiders and so on.

To extend the activity for older children you could ask them to work in pairs and then to write down the name of the pairs they have sent the Bee-Bot to 'collect' in five or ten minutes using a sand or wind up timer.

## Storybook activity

After listening to a suitable storybook with which the children are familiar (perhaps, *The Pig in the Pond*, *We're Going on a Bear Hunt* or *Whatever Next!*) encourage them to draw some of the characters or events onto the squares on the sheets. These can be in any square the children decide, just fill some not all of the squares. Then decide on a starting square and encourage the children to write the word 'start' onto this and also 'end' on an end square. If necessary the adult can scribe for the children.

Place the Bee-Bot board over the prepared sheet matching up the squares grid if necessary. The children can now send the Bee-Bot to the events of the story in the sequence they occur. This may involve them discussing or referring to the book to clarify their thinking.

Once they have been made, these sheets can be used again and again, and of course this type of activity supports literacy and much more.

## Number activity

Draw a number line on the squared grid and then place the Bee-Bot board over the prepared sheet, matching up the squares markings if necessary. Use this to send the Bee-Bot along the number line. Then later extend the activity to work out how many 'steps' it takes between numbers for example, between 2 and 7 the answer would be 5.

There are many commercially produced activity ideas books for the Bee-Bot and there is also software available for use on PCs and IWBs as well as tunnels and mazes.

# Ipad/tablet

This is a relatively new piece of ICT hardware but one which children from as young as two are starting to engage with some success. There are many free or low cost apps that can be downloaded depending on the age of the children.

There are many to choose from, and the list is growing every week, but here are a few you might want to consider. You will need to try them out first to make sure they are suitable for the age of your children and their learning needs.

- **Talking Tom**
- **Talking Pierre**
- **Talking Santa**
- **Bubble Ball Free**
- **4 in a row**
- **Merry Xmas**
- **Go Count**
- **Edu Kitchen**

- **Kid's Find the Shadow**
- **Picture book for toddler**
- **Chipper's Challenge**
- **Words**
- **Tiny Zoo Friends**
- **Bee-Bot**
- **Tracing ABC**
- **Compass**

- **Virtuoso- piano**
- **Magic Piano**
- **Glow draw**
- **Math monkey**
- **Princess**
- **Mix and match**

# Interactive whiteboards (IWBs)

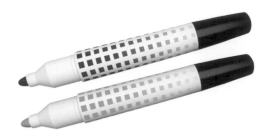

IWBs and large touch screens enable groups of children to share a visual image at the same time and as a result share interactive and shared learning. IWBs or smart boards have increasingly become a part of early years provision in schools, day nurseries and children's centres. They are a useful teaching tool because they offer a very large and visual dimension as well as promoting:

■ **opportunities for collaborative/small group work**

■ **accessibility for all but especially for children with some visual and/or physical impairment**

■ **opportunity for interacting and being active**

■ **recording, saving and storing information**

■ **linking to other devices such as ipads or cameras (including webcams).**

There is an alternative to IWBs which is now affordable – namely the large touch screens and these should be considered because:

◆ **of health and safety considerations relating to children being in front of (or accidentally looking into) a potentially damaging beam from a projector**

◆ **they are easier for children to use and can be cleaned of finger prints more easily than an IWB**

◆ **they can be very easily fitted at a suitable children's height**

◆ **pricewise they are similar to the costs of the IWB and in some cases slightly cheaper.**

One aspect to be wary of is that IWBs or large touch screens can, if practitioners are not careful, lead down the road to a more didactic teaching model and away from the more play based/active learning model promoted by the revised EYFS.

IWBs and large touch screens support learning in multi modal ways because they allow for:

● **visualisation and reflection**

● **communication and shared or collaborative extension of ideas**

● **representations and organisation of ideas**

● **more divergent teaching and learning strategies**

● **interaction with the display.**

To ensure that when practitioners are using an IWB or large touch screen the teaching is of a high quality there must be opportunities within the planned session for children to:

→ **engage in a task which puts them in control**

→ **work collaboratively**

→ **be supported and guided in their collaboration work by a practitioner or a more able peer and so engage in higher thinking levels**

→ **engage in a group learning situation which allows them to be a real participant of that group.**

It is unlikely that a whole-class session will enable children to get the most out of the learning opportunities on offer. So it is advisable to split the group into smaller learning groups to take full advantage of what the technology provides. We know that smaller groups give children the opportunity to engage more and speak more and this knowledge should again help to guide our thinking as to the optimum size of groupings.

# Chapter 6

# Inclusion and early ICT

> ❝ **Inclusion is a process of identifying, understanding and breaking down barriers to participation.**
>
> *National Early Years Forum* 2004 ❞

Inclusion starts with changing attitudes towards what children can really do when barriers to their participation are eliminated. It is about understanding what the needs of all the children in the group are and making sure that no child is disadvantaged due to issues around access.

Early ICT can be extremely supportive in making access to learning possible for all children, by ensuring that every child's learning needs styles and motivations are carefully observed, monitored and responded to in effective ways. Part of this can be using ICT to help children to focus their attention and allow independent use of equipment and resources, thus allowing the child as learner to be in control and to develop at their own pace. Because ICT is so motivational for many children it can interest them in engaging in a wide range of opportunities to learn in different ways. Inclusion involving ICT applications is about recognising what children could do if their needs and interests are met. Hence it is essential to recognise 'the unique child' in every child and to consider how their needs, interests and abilities can be supported and stimulated through ICT.

Inclusion through ICT is about the provision of meaningful ICT experiences which are:

- **the entitlement of every child**

- **an essential and key part of the provision offered.**

IOT should be used to enable practitioners to more effectively:

- ■ **challenge stereotypes and develop positive images of young children with physical or learning diabilities and others in the community**

- ■ **engage, motivate and inspire children**

- ■ **support all aspects across the seven areas of learning both indoors and outdoors**

- ■ **support exploration, experimentation and independent learning**

- ■ **promote, support and extend child-initiated learning.**

Inclusive ICT will provide rich and meaningful opportunities for all children for:

- ◆ **extending learning opportunities beyond what was previously available**

- ◆ **stimulation and intrinsic enjoyment**

- ◆ **the development of physical skills**

- ◆ **engagement at higher levels and for longer periods**

- ◆ **the development of independence**

- ◆ **the dynamic expression of emotions, feelings, opinion and personality**

- ◆ **the characteristics of effective learning to be developed, supported and displayed.**

(Adapted from BECTA guidelines & EYFS Guidance)

# Children with Special Educational Needs and Disabilities (SEND)

> " The EYFS seeks to provide ... equality of opportunity and anti-discriminatory practice, ensuring that every child is included and supported. "
>
> *Statutory Framework for the Early Years Foundation Stage* 2012

Many children with SEND will particularly benefit from the provision and use of ICT if they are provided with adaptations which enable them to access learning. Wherever necessary, or desirable, specialist advice or support should be sought about adaptations that can be made and then acted upon. Adapted activities should be provided, such as enabling a child who is confined to a wheelchair to use a remote control toy car by providing an elevated area so they can comfortably reach the toy.

Differentiated activities should also be provided either through the level available within the software or through access devices such as buttons or switches. Consideration must, where appropriate, be given to providing specialised or modified resources and equipment such as:

★ **speech output communication aids**

★ **audio links from computers of IWBs to hearing aid loop systems**

★ **keyboards with larger keys**

★ **roller ball mice**

★ **tactile switch**

★ **large light up switch**

★ **speech responsive software**

★ **enlarging text icons and providing speech facilities for children with impaired vision, such as within a talking word processor.**

## Space around equipment

An important consideration is to always provide sufficient space around all equipment and devices so that children with mobility needs, including wheelchair and special seat users, can be positioned to see the screen and access the keyboards or other input devices. This is a key part of your access strategy. Remember that trailing wires can be dangerous for all children but especially those identified with SEND so these should all be removed or tidied away. As ICT will be located around so many areas of the indoor and outdoor environment this will be a consideration across your whole environment.

# ICT and children for whom English is an additional language (EAL)

> For children whose home language is not English, providers must take reasonable steps to provide opportunities for children to develop and use their home language in play and learning ... Providers must also ensure that children have sufficient opportunities to learn and reach a good standard in English...
>
> *Statutory Framework for the Early Years Foundation Stage* 2012

Some EAL children will be bilingual, having been spoken to in two languages since birth, but many others will still be developing fluency in their home language alone. In order for children to develop skills in using any language they need to feel relaxed, secure and safe and to understand that the way they speak and their culture is accepted and valued. We know from research that there is a strong link between language and identity and that learning is most effective when practitioners build on what children already know and can do.

It is important that whatever we plan and provide for children for whom English is not their first language builds on this and provides planned opportunities for speaking and listening through activities that are appropriately matched to their cognitive abilities. ICT can provide many opportunities for EAL children to develop their understanding through activities that make use of visual, contextual and linguistic support. Those who work with EAL children in the EYFS can use ICT effectively to support them by:

★ **being aware that children will often understand more than they are able to say; especially when supported by non verbal communication such as gesture, facial expression and other visual or pictorial aids**

★ **providing well planned interactive activities where speaking and listening have a high profile**

★ **maximising bilingual support**

★ **recognising the importance of children seeing and hearing their home language, as well as English, in the learning environment.**

Children should be encouraged to use their first or home language where possible such as in writing or recording for a photograph book. This will help to encourage children and their parents or carers that this is important and also reinforce the fact that fluency in the child's home language will support the acquisitions of an additional language as well as providing cognitive benefits.

Practitioners need to understand that children will have already developed concepts in their home language although they may not yet as yet be able to demonstrate this in English. Opportunities should therefore be provided for children to demonstrate their understanding through practical, hands-on use of ICT resources and equipment which can support observational based assessment for learning.

## Giving children a voice

Increasingly it is being recognised that we cannot get a true picture of the child without having the perspectives of:

● **practitioners**

● **parents and carers**

● **the child.**

It is often more difficult to involve children in the process of consultation and discussion about what is provided for them than to involve their parents and carers and practitioners.

Non-computer based equipment can provide us with a 'way in' to hearing the child's voice but also gives us a support mechanism for encouraging the child's voice to be heard. The views of EAL children are often particularly difficult to access. We know that if we provide meaningful learning activities and experiences we are likely to see engagement from more children.

ICT can be highly effective in capturing and recording how children and their parents and carers have been consulted. Digital images (still and moving) taken by a child allow us to see the provision and the perspective of their world through their eyes. We should consider involving in our work consultations with children and 'listening' to their perspectives through the use of equipment such as cameras and voice recorders. Giving children the opportunity, the encouragement and support to communicate their perspective can be eye opening for practitioners. Often children will choose to record their perspective outdoors and this is not at all surprising given that both the use of ICT resources and learning outdoors promote greater confidence with communication. (Bilton et al 1990)

## Essential equipment

When asked which items of ICT I would have in my setting above all else I always say:

■ a child friendly digital camera

■ a karaoke machine.

Those who have these in their provision will recognise many reasons why I say this but some of the most important reasons are that they:

→ **excite and motivate children**

→ **encourage communication and speaking and listening skills**

→ **particularly encourage boys to engage with them, as well as girls**

→ **are transparent in their use and easy to use**

→ **encourage and support sustained shared thinking**

→ **promote social interaction.**

I now have a new addition to these two – the voice changer. Staff I have worked with recently have found it amazing how such a simple device can and does change how children behave. Many of those young children who were very self-conscious and reluctant to speak, or who spoke in whispers, were suddenly transformed and became much noisier and less passive. They appeared to enjoy hearing their voice sounding so different and as a result for a few minutes they became different too!

The longer term effect was also amazing as the quiet children grew louder and more confident and began to have more of a 'voice' in other situations. Eventually they didn't need the voice changer to 'hide behind' as much although they still enjoyed engaging with it.

# Chapter 7

# Early ICT case studies

> **Children today are born into a technological world and there is a great deal practitioners in settings can do to make the most of the new opportunities which technology now offers.**
>
> *Gould* 2012

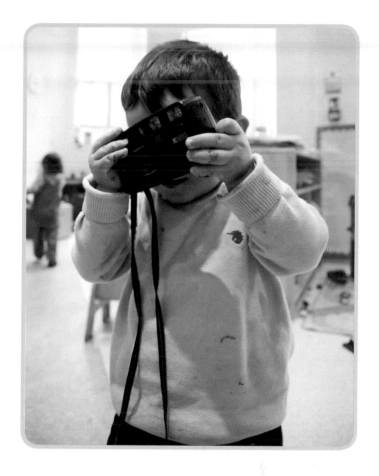

## Case study 1

## Using a digital camera

This case study looks at opportunities to support learning and teaching in Communication and Language in the EYFS in a Manchester day nursery.

The availability and use of digital cameras has grown rapidly over the past few years. As practitioners at this nursery setting have become more familiar and confident in operating them it has opened up new horizons for their effective use in the setting, so as to support learning and teaching and improved outcomes for children.

One major benefit of using digital cameras noted by practitioners was that the existing learning environment, both indoors and outdoors, was used to greater effect and extended beyond the physical restraints of the actual building and its immediate surroundings.

Children had been observed learning to use visual images long before they learned to read and write. For example, most children attending the setting were able to recognise the local McDonald's sign. This setting decided to take up a new approach to using digital cameras, recognising that the use of digital images could be the key to using the expertise and understanding some of the children already had. In this way they felt it might build their self-esteem and enjoyment of the learning process while at the same time integrating cross-curricular learning that incorporated ICT.

The previous experience of two members of staff was that using digital cameras had been shown to offer collaborative learning opportunities with a medium that is increasingly important, and very likely to impact on the rest of the child's life.

Working in the ways outlined in this case study has not only helped to keep the children at the centre of what is provided but have also given practitioners an insight into how children perceive themselves, others and their surrounding world.

Some of the advantages of using digital cameras in this setting were identified as:

- empowering children to develop essential life skills

- having an end product and a process which is quickly and easily accessible

- using an adaptable and exciting piece of technology which captivates children's interests and motivates them as learners

- providing evidence of achievement and curriculum coverage

- producing images which are a stimulation for learning.

Additionally they can be used to:

- support learning and teaching through aiding the production of stimulating learning resources

- support parents' understanding of assessment for learning

- enrich and extend displays within the learning environment

- enable children to enhance their learning

- make books with the children

- ensure the learning environment reflects the children much more through the use of photos of them engaged in exciting child-initiated and adult-led activities

- provide evidence of learning that would be impossible to record otherwise

- identify effective routes into improved work with children involving speaking and listening and reading and writing.

The following examples of a digital camera in use within the setting show the rich, cross curricular, learning opportunities which supported working towards the Early Learning Goals in the areas of: Communication and Language, Literacy and Knowledge of the World.

## Storytime

During the week the children had been listening to the story of 'The Gingerbread Man' which was a favourite book for many of them and they had been encouraged to join in with some of the words. The adult used a digital camera from the pictures in the book to create an image of the characters that the Gingerbread Man met on his journey.

The adult then worked with the children to use the photographs to recall the correct order in which the characters were encountered, which ultimately ended with meeting the fox and crossing the river.

The activity was recorded using a webcam set up close by. The children were helped to recall and sequence the events of the story through the use of these images. Later the images were used to create a book with the children which retold the story in their own words through the adult scribing.

At a group time the next day, the children watched the video clip which had been recorded on the webcam through the IWB and the adult was able to talk with the children and recap on the activity.

Later the children were able to access the video clip themselves through the PC and the IWB. It created a great deal of interest from the children and many parents asked if they could look at the clip after children excitedly told their families about it.

## An autumn walk

In the autumn term children went on a walk into their local environment, which was close to a canal. During this trip they were encouraged to look closely at the surrounding environment and talk with the adult about what they could see, touch, smell and hear.

The practitioners and children took photographs, using a digital camera with a memory stick, as a record of the trip. The children were encouraged to talk about why they had chosen to take each picture and this was recorded using a digital voice recorder.

On returning to school the photographs were downloaded and imported into a PowerPoint presentation with the appropriate recorded language added to individual pictures. This was made available for the children to view as a slide show through the IWB and also printed out and made into a book.

Some of the digital images selected by the children were put through the IWB and the adult acted as a scribe, recording what the children wanted to say about the images. These images and the text decided on by the children were again saved onto a DVD, printed out, and then made into a book for the book area.

A laminated picture of an interesting bridge seen and photographed during the walk was placed in the construction area and a challenge set up for the children: 'Can you build a bridge like this?'

Items that the children collected during their walk, and photographs of the children collecting some of these, were placed in the investigation area. Children later used information books to identify the type of tree from which the conkers, pine cones and some of the leaves had come. The adults supported this and helped to model and reinforce appropriate language, helping to embed this within the children's cognitive understanding.

These images were thus used to:

◆ **talk about things they had seen on the walk**

◆ **create books about the walk**

◆ **create a slide show of the walk, with sounds of the children talking about their pictures**

◆ **provide support and stimulus for children to use their creative skills to make representational models of some of the interesting structures they had seen on the trip, including a bridge.**

## Using small world resources

After a visit to a local farm children were supported and encouraged, in small groups, by the adults to set up storyboard type scenarios of a farm based story, using a range of familiar resources available in the small world area, and to share a non-fiction book about farm animals. With support from the adult, they took a series of photographs of things the small world animals were doing using a digital camera.

The children photographed a horse eating real hay, a horse jumping over a fence, cows eating grass, pigs rolling in the mud and a pig launching into a shallow pond.

With the help of the adult the children downloaded the images, printed these out and made them into a book. They contributed their own words about the images, with the adults scribing these for them underneath the pictures. The completed book was shared with other children at group time and was later used by the children as a shared focus for talk.

Later in the outdoor area, a group of children were playing imaginatively with a range of child sized builder's yard tools and equipment – including a digger and a dumper truck. Supported by the adult children took a series of photographs of action taking place in the 'builders yard'. They talked about what was happening in each of the scenes photographed and the adult scribed what the children actually said. Later the images were downloaded into a PowerPoint presentation and printed out with what the children said under each image. Books were made of the images and words spoken. The children later shared these books with other children and their parents when they came to collect them.

## Making and using a number line

In the nursery the practitioners took photographs of the children, printed them out and laminated them, then made these into a number line. The numbers were fastened to the line with clothes pegs. Number 1 had a photograph of one child, number 2 had a photograph of two children and so on.

The children were encouraged to talk about the number line and which children were used to represent each number.

Each day for the next week, before the children arrived, the puppet 'Foxy' took away one of the numbers during the night and the children were asked if they could guess which number Foxy had hidden.

Then a note from Foxy was read out explaining where he had hidden it.

A child's name was then picked out of the decorated names box and the child with a chosen friend went to find it. If they found it difficult the rest of the group were asked to give them clues to help. Some of the children when asked were able to remember the children on the missing number card.

Through this use of the digital camera children's interest in a number line was increased and their skills in recognising and understanding the number line sequence was supported.

## Using puppets

In the nursery one of the practitioners frequently used a large hand puppet of a dog to good effect during the group times. The puppet was named Blackie and was a great favourite with the children.

One day the practitioner brought in a book from home, which she had made about her dog, called Billy. She had titled the book 'Where is Billy?' and read it to the children. She suggested that perhaps they could together make a book 'Where is Blackie?'.

A small group of interested children worked with the practitioner to make a book. The children chose five places in the room where Blackie could not be found. Photographs were taken of these five places and then finally a photograph was taken of a sixth place where the children decided Blackie was to be found.

Working with the adult and using the book 'Where is Billy?' as a model the children used the printed out digital images to make their own book which they shared with others in the class. Each photograph was made into a page with appropriately repeating words being used. On the first page it read:

'Is Blackie in the book area?

No, he is not there.'

And so on until the final page where it read

'Is Blackie in the growing area?

Yes, there he is lying down in front of the plants!'

This home made book was then shared with the other children and placed in the book area for children to access independently.

## In conclusion

The potential use of digital cameras offers a wide range of opportunities to support learning and teaching. Many more ideas can be thought of for, with or by the children. For those looking for a wealth of instant ideas Helen Bromley has produced a book *Picture This: 50 Exciting Ways to Use a Camera in Early Years Settings* (2003 Lawrence Educational Publications) that will help EYFS practitioners to among other things:

- **integrate ICT across all areas of the curriculum**

- **offer innovative ways to involve speaking and listening and reading and writing which will engage and motivate children**

- **promote and encourage the development of speaking and listening skills**

- **excite and motivate children to find learning fun**

- **help to interest and involve parents in meaningful ways in their children's learning and development.**

## Case study 2

# Using desktop software

> **Children use their storying as a tool for thinking as they explore thought, ideas and feelings and what they know about.**
>
> *Rich D. 2002*

Children have much more to say than practitioners often think and this is exemplified through this case study which shows how, through the use of desktop software, children can be supported and encouraged to create their own real and imaginary stories.

This case study took place with a range of young children aged three to five years in Manchester settings. The practitioners and children who engaged with the project were supported by an advisory teacher who visited over a period of six weeks.

The idea was to test the value and outcomes of young children being helped to tell their own stories which would be recorded by the adult (using the 'write' software from Tizzy's First Tool) and played back so children could listen to what they had created. It was inspired by the work of Whitehead (2009) who wrote of 'the value of encouraging young children to tell their own stories' and so empowering their creative voice.

The adult worked with the child as a 'literacy partner' making it possible for them to create print for a real purpose. With the adult acting as scribe, the burden of transcription is taken away and the child is free to focus on the content of their storytelling. The project demonstrated the communicative and inspirational power of the written word and some of the more 'invisible' aspects of authorship.

Children told stories about different things which were important and significant to them. As their stories were written and printed there appeared to be some intangible kind of magic for the children that continued to grow as they recognised that they could share their story many times with others.

Daniel wrote a short story about the place where he lives:

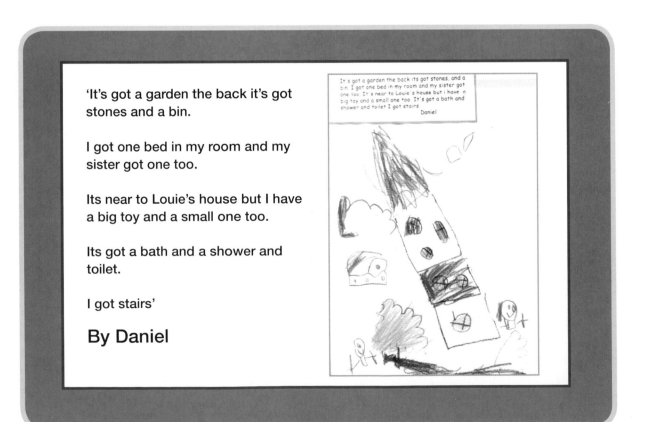

'It's got a garden the back it's got stones and a bin.

I got one bed in my room and my sister got one too.

Its near to Louie's house but I have a big toy and a small one too.

Its got a bath and a shower and toilet.

I got stairs'

**By Daniel**

Other children wrote familiar stories in their own words like Hamze's about Ninja Turtles:

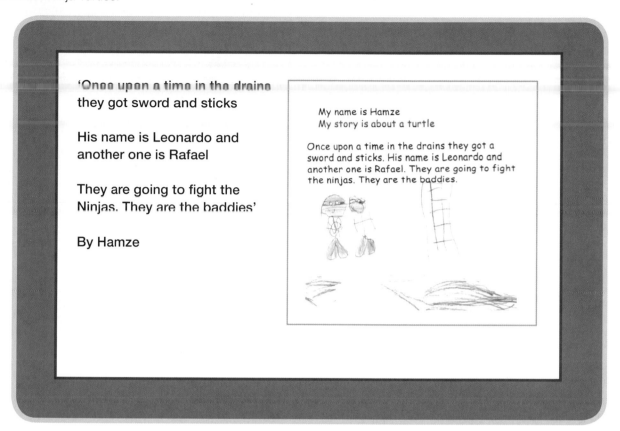

'Once upon a time in the drains they got sword and sticks

His name is Leonardo and another one is Rafael

They are going to fight the Ninjas. They are the baddies'

By Hamze

My name is Hamze
My story is about a turtle

Once upon a time in the drains they got a sword and sticks. His name is Leonardo and another one is Rafael. They are going to fight the ninjas. They are the baddies.

Other children were inspired by familiar storybooks. In the case of Umaira it was 'Goldilocks and the Three Bears':

'Once upon a time there were three bears. Mummy Bear, Baby Bear and Daddy Bear.

Mummy Bear said 'lets go for a walk in the woods ' Then there was someone else in the woods . Her name was Goldilocks and she said' I wonder who lives at that house?' and she knocked on the door and no one wasn't there. So she stepped in and saw three porriages. First she tried the Daddy Bear's. And she said ' Ugh too hot' Then she tried the mummy bears. Then she tried the Baby Bear's .Then she saw three chairs. Then she tried the three chairs. Then she sat on Daddy Bears chair, then she sat on Mummy Bear's chair. Then she sat on the Baby Bears chair and that was the right one then she broked it. Then she saw the three bears beds.First she saw saw Daddy Bears bed. She sleeped in it. Then she sleeped in Mummy Dears Ded.....'

By Umaira

In each of these three stories the practitioners recorded the written text exactly as the child said it. This draws attention to the child's developmental use of language and provides a record of this. It is clear that in Umaira's case she has been influenced by good quality stories being read to her and shared with her. She shows herself able to recall many details of the story – and retell these in her own way – many of which are taken directly from the original story.

The children were encouraged to tell their stories to the computer. As the adult typed the words the children said, they highlighted the text and the computer was able to 'read' this back using the voice function. This helped to motivate the children to tell more and then to listen to what had been written on an ongoing basis as their stories developed. The effect of this was to make a clear connection for the child between the spoken and the written word.

Many stories were written during the project and the final one shared in this case study is one by Crystal who used her imaginative and expressive abilities to show just how much she knew about the world and how it operates around holidays and travel.

In creating this story, the practitioner and Crystal were involved in a great deal of shared discussions and raising questions such as what kind of orange juice it was or the colour of the cheese. This process enabled Crystal to further develop her descriptive skills which gives an added dimension to her story.

'Once upon a time there was a little mouse going to the seaside on a bus. He got off and went on an aeroplane and people were stamping on him. They couldn't see him because he was too tiny.

He escaped when the aeroplane arrived and landed and he went on a coach, a single decker one, to Wales so he could stay there for a bit, half a day. He went to sleep in a hotel and when he woke up for breakfast he had some yellow cheese and orange juice and it was fizzy. After his breakfast he fell asleep and watched telly when he woke up. Ten it was time to go back to the place where he belongs in England. Back on the coach, back on the aeroplane, into his mousehole and straight to bed

The End

By Crystal

Clearly the role of the practitioner is helping children to get started in their storytelling and differentiating the activity so that each child could achieve according to their stage of development and their interest level.

Key findings of the project, identified by the staff were that the use of the software enabled children to:

→ **see the connections between their thoughts, the words they spoke and the words written**

→ **listen to their inner voice and thoughts and say and record these**

→ **see the use of writing and its lasting quality compared to talk**

→ **see the practitioner writing and enjoying it**

→ **write real stories which enabled them to unlock their ideas and see themselves as real authors.**

The overall success and impact of the project was that it bred further success for the children as story makers and unlocked a willingness in them to participate in a range of other writing opportunities away from the computer such as in the writing area and the role-play area. The software seems to have enabled the practitioners to make the learning accessible, motivational and enjoyable for the children. Many children exceeded expectations in the project, demonstrating that for some children ICT can help to unlock their true potential in ways that other resources do not.

## Case study 3

# Using metal detectors

This case study illustrates how a nursery class used metal detectors in an exciting project to support language and social skills. A nursery class in Southport has a large outdoor sandpit in which, among other things, many of the children like to dig. They use spades to make sandcastles and imaginatively play with large dinosaurs and big dumper trucks. In the summer term, following on from a noted interest brought in by the children, a mini topic on pirates was embraced and the children were very much immersed in being pirates.

### Pirate project

One of the children decided to be Bluebeard the pirate and lead his company of pirates to capture treasure and bury this in the sand to be dug up later. After some discussion with the practitioners, it was decided that the pirates would need a map to locate which treasure was buried where. Large sheets of thick decorator's lining paper was used for the maps and these were made to look old and authentic by staining with old tea bags and being torn at the edges. The children worked in groups adding marks to the map to indicate where each piece of treasure was buried. Then they decided to have another

'trip to sea' to capture a rich ship and take its treasure before coming back for the treasure they had buried which was silver, gold and jewels.

Once they returned from their trip, they used the map they had made to try to find the buried treasure but only managed to find eight out of the 12 pieces as the sand was very deep. Then Bluebeard had the idea of using the hand-held metal detector they had been using in the investigation area to sort metal objects from those not made of metal. Soon the children managed to find all the rest of the treasure using the metal detector. They noted when it beeped louder then dug up close to where there was the strongest beep.

Two days later the keys for the shed were lost just before home time and there was a feeling that they may have fallen into the long grass. When they could not be found quickly one of the children suggested that the adult used the large metal detector to try to find the keys. To the delight of all concerned, and to the relief of the adults, the keys were located and the shed could be locked safely for the night.

The next day the children decided to play 'burying' the treasure in the long grass and finding it using the metal detector and much fun was had by all.

As the nursery is close to a local beach several more sensitive metal detectors were purchased and a trip organised for a small group of children to go treasure troving on the beach. Lots of rusty iron pieces were found but one child found an old gold ring and another found an old brooch. This started some children becoming very interested in going metal troving at home with their families.

## Case study 4

# Using Easi-phones

Some of the children at Alma Park school in Manchester found walkie-talkies difficult to use so staff there have recently invested in a number of user friendly mini mobile phones called Easi-phones for their EYFS children. The name Easi-phone describes them well as they are very easy for young children to use

The Easi-phones proved to be an instant hit with the children who were very interested in 'smart' phones and who loved to imitate the adults in their lives. Rita Bannon, the nursery teacher, found that the children were quickly able to use these devices independently, initially needing only the minimum of adult support. They sparked off conversations that otherwise would not have taken place like this between Shahid and Marie

Shahid   *"What you doing?"*

Marie   *"I'm being a builder outside. I'm making a house"*

Shahid   *"Hello hello... I can see you and now I can hear you."*

Marie   *"Where are you?"*

Shahid   *"In the play house making a cup of coffee... Do you want one?"*

Marie   *"Yes please, I'm coming in now for it"*

Rita, along with many other early years practitioners, had become increasingly concerned about some children's delayed or limited speaking and listening skills. She felt that these devices could help to provide the opportunities needed to help focus and develop these prime communication skills.

All the staff noted how much the Easi-phones inspired children to speak and listen. They also provided excellent opportunities to support other areas of the curriculum such as PD, PSED as well as KW using everyday ICT. Rita explained that on the day they arrived children were using them independently within a very short period.

The experiences from Alma Park have been replicated in many other settings and staff there are very confident that the phones will continue to be used and not relegated to a cupboard shelf once the novelty has worn off.

# Appendix 1 Early ICT Basic Skills and Knowledge Assessment Audit Record

| Emerging interest and awareness | Learning to operating basic ICT toys and resources | Operates simple ICT toys and resources | Operates programmable ICT toys and devices | Assessment and next steps |
|---|---|---|---|---|
| Shows interest in toys/ resources with buttons flaps and mechanisms | Learning to turn on and operate some basic ICT based toys and equipment | Can operates simple remote control car or other device/s | Operates more advanced toys/ devices e.g remote control, talking tins, metal detector, Easi-phone | |
| Anticipates repeated sounds and actions when use of an action toy is being repeated by an adult | Learning to operate simple mechanical toys e.g turns knob or winds up toy or pulls back on friction care | Can turn on CD player or radio using switch/ knob | Can retrieve information on a computer e.g from 'my documents' or 'my pictures' | |
| | | Can use remote control handset to turn on device eg television CD player | Completes a simple program on a computer/i-pad | |
| | | Shows an interest in /talks about technological toys and devices such as camera, talking Santa, mobile phone and keen to start to operate these | Able to programme a Bee-bot, Pixie or Roamer to move using up to five instructions | |
| | | Operates a still camera at a basic level | Navigates through a range of internet programs | |
| | | Uses mouse or other control switch to access/operate software | Navigates through a range of software programs | |
| | | | Operates a movie/dvd camera at a basic level | |
| | | | Able to programme a Beebot, Pixie or Roamer to move using more than five instructions | |
| | | | Recognises and talks about how technology is used eg home/ nursery/school | |
| | | | Selects and uses technology for a specific purpose e.g. metal detector to find lost keys or coins | |

# Appendix 2

## Useful websites

There are a wide range of useful websites available for use with early years children, including:

www.bbc.co.uk/schools/websites/preschool

www.bbc.co.uk/schools/numbertime

www.bbc.co.uk/cbeebies search for Teletubbies, Tweenies, Fimbles, Balamory and more.

www.bgfl.org/bgfl/primary.cfm/earlyyears

www.funwithspot.com/uk

www.sesameworkshop.org

http://pbskids.org

www.themouseclub.co.uk

www.bobthebuilder.com

 www.poissonrouge.com

http://www.thomasandfriends.com

http://nickjr.co.uk/shows/dora

# Appendix 3

## Useful software

Some excellent early years software available includes:

**Tizzy's First Tools** by Sherston/RM Education a fully integrated set of seven ICT tools (write/paint/publish/move/chart/decide/present) designed for children aged four plus.

**The Mouse Club Shop** (www.themouseclub.co.uk/shop) from d2 Digital by Design Limited has a range of early years programs including: *Mouse In The House, Mouse Island, Mouse Music, Mouse Studio, Who Ate the Cheese?* and *Special Me.*

**Sherston software** has: *ABC CD – Talking Animated Alphabet, Fizzy's First Numbers, Nursery Rhyme Time, Young MacDonald's Farm, Polka Dot Park (Materials, Habitats, Growth), The Not So Naughty Stories, At the Café, At the Post Office, Rainbow Street, My Modelling Toolkit 1, Making Creatures, Sound Beginnings 1, Sound Beginnings 2.*

**2Simple** has: *Simple City, Alphabet Soup, Maths City 1, Maths City 2, 2Create a Story.*

# Bibliography and further reading

*Development Matters in the Early Years Foundation Stage* (Early Education 2012)

*Statutory Framework for the Early Years Foundation Stage* (Department for Education, 2012)

Bilton Helen et al (1990) *Learning Outdoors – Improving the Quality of Young Children's Play Outdoors* (Letts)

Siraj-Blatchford Iram and Siraj-Blatchford John (2003) *More Than Computers: Information and Communication Technology in the Early Years Early Education*

Siraj-Blatchford John and Whitebread David (2003) *Supporting ICT in the Early Years* (Open University Press)

Bromley Helen (2003) *Picture This: 50 Exciting Ways to Use a Camera in Early Years Settings* (Lawrence Educational Publications)

Cooper Bridget and Brna Paul (2002) *Hidden Curriculum, Hidden Feelings: Emotions, Relationships and Learning with ICT and the Whole Child* Conference Paper BERA

O'Hara Mark (2004) *ICT in the Early Years* (Continuum International Press)

Price Harriet (2008) *The Really Useful Book of ICT in the Early Years* (Routledge Education)

Rich D (2002) *More than words - Children developing communication, language and literacy* (Early Education)

Whitehead Marion (2009) *Supporting Language and Literacy Development in the Early Years* (Open University Press)

Woodbridge J (2002) Presentation to delegates at The Early Excellence Centre Huddersfield

PRESS IT, SWITCH IT, TURN IT, MOVE IT!